YOUR KNOWLEDGE HAS VALUE

- We will publish your bachelor's and master's thesis, essays and papers

- Your own eBook and book - sold worldwide in all relevant shops

- Earn money with each sale

Upload your text at www.GRIN.com
and publish for free

The Meaning of Violence in Shakespeare's "Titus Andronicus"

Bibliographic information published by the German National Library:

The German National Library lists this publication in the National Bibliography; detailed bibliographic data are available on the Internet at http://dnb.dnb.de.

ISBN: 9783389022351
This book is also available as an ebook.

© GRIN Publishing GmbH
Trappentreustraße 1
80339 München

Print and binding: Books on Demand GmbH, Norderstedt, Germany
Printed on acid-free paper from responsible sources.

The present work has been carefully prepared. Nevertheless, authors and publishers do not incur liability for the correctness of information, notes, links and advice as well as any printing errors.

GRIN web shop: https://www.grin.com/document/1458203

Friedrich-Alexander-Universität Erlangen-Nürnberg

Department of English and American Studies

WiSe 2020/2021

The Meaning of Violence in Shakespeare's Titus Andronicus

Table of Contents

1 The History of Violence

In Shakespeare's early work *Titus Andronicus*, fourteen people meet their deaths on stage through various forms of murder and mutilation, desecration and involuntary cannibalism. Here, after a war with the Romans and Goths, two violent cultures collide. After the Gothic queen Tamora - although she was actually the spoils of war of the Romans - is taken as a wife by their new emperor, she and her lover take revenge for the ritual murder of one of her sons by the Romans. Now a spiral of violence is inexorably turning, to which she also falls victim.

Since the beginning of human history and since myths and legends have existed, man, especially the male sex, has committed acts of violence. Violence here means physical and psychological coercion against people, and all actions that harm animals or things. Obviously, our instincts cause us to defend ourselves in certain situations. There are various reasons for this, e.g. to protect oneself, the family or the tribe from attackers, or to gain prestige and thus a higher social status. If we accept the fact that violence is something natural, we should also be open to stories and literary works that deal with this topic. So we should not condemn it, but try to understand it and learn to deal with this human tendency.[1] The fact that outbreaks of violence have taken place - and are still taking place - in all kinds of forms and in all kinds of narratives or religions all over the world and at all times shows that human instincts and behaviors have been passed on. The reasons always seem to have the same basis, namely to protect the people and the weaker ones, to gain new land or property.[2] In the world of Titus Andronicus, the motives for the numerous murders include revenge, anger, hatred, jealousy, pride, ambition and envy.

Since the inclination to violence is particularly rooted in man's nature and is also triggered by social constructions, he has probably always had to struggle with an urge to do so throughout history and learn to control this urge. In the Elizabethan age, spectators of drama enjoyed public spectacles of torture and violence. Where people would look away today, many enjoyed it then and found it in: "the execution of criminals and traitors staged as ceremonies validating state power or in the punishment by whipping until blood flowed that could be inflicted on fornicators by ecclesiastical courts."[3] A quote from Michel de Montaigne expresses this state of affairs in a very appropriate way:

> I could hardly be persuaded, before I had seen it, that the world could have afforded so marble-hearted and savage minded men, that for the only pleasure of murder would commit it, then cut, mangle, and hack other members in pieces: to rouse and sharpen their wits, to invent unused tortures and unheard-of torments; to devise new and unknown deaths and that in cold

---

[1] R. A. Foakes, *Shakespeare and Violence*. Cambridge: Cambridge UP, 2003, 1.
[2] Foakes, *Shakespeare and Violence*, 2.
[3] Foakes, *Shakespeare and Violence*, 36.

3

blood, without any former enmity or quarrel, or without any gain or profit; and only to this end, that they enjoy the pleasing spectacle of the languishing gestures, pitiful motions, horror-moving yelling, deep fetched groans, and lamentable voices of a dying and drooping man.[4]

Why is it not immoral to wage war and kill people, while on the other hand it is immoral to kill people outside a battlefield? Most people find that wars are part of our society. Behind this is the idea that violence in this context is for self-defense. It is not only accepted but also highly respected to have the *courage* to kill someone who is attacking you, your family or your country. This is the case with Titus Andronicus, the Roman general who returns to Rome victorious from the war against the Goths at the beginning of the eponymous work and is celebrated and highly respected for it.

Many agree that violence and bloodshed are inherently negative and morally wrong, but that they can also do something positive in the context of war. Although killing and violence are never right, they are often necessary in today's world. When you look at world history and think back to all the devastating wars and battles, you wonder if violence and bloodshed can ever be moral. Of course it is wrong to intentionally inflict pain or take the life of another human being, regardless of what that person has done before. The belief that one should not kill is common throughout the world and in all major world religions. Nevertheless, there are often circumstances in which violence may be necessary. Be it to prevent a great evil or to repay someone for what they have done to you. The question here is where to draw the line. What justifies violence? Is it justified to take human life because there is an official war going on? If a son is killed in front of his mother, is it okay for the mother to take revenge? Is it okay for a father to kill his daughter's rapists? The problem is that we have to compare the value of different human lives when making such decisions. However, one could argue that it is equally wrong to simply stand by and do nothing in the face of evil. Perhaps it is possible to find meaning in the cruelty displayed on stage, and perhaps it is also possible to make a statement about the society we live in today through this work. As you can see, Titus Andronicus explores violence from different angles that we can look at. We are shown that in this play civilization and barbarism are not at odds with each other, but that barbarism is at the heart of civilization. By focusing on Shakespeare's Titus Andronicus, I intend to discuss the question of what motivates people to commit acts of violence. What passions and which social emotions lead to violence in Shakespeare's Titus Andronicus. I want to show that the events of the work are not too distant from us, but that perhaps each of us is

---

[4] Michel Montaigne, *Of Cruelty*, 1580; in: Foakes, *Shakespeare and Violence*, v.

capable of committing violence. After all, when Tamora first appears, she is portrayed as a victim and one has no idea that a woman who weeps like this for her son is capable of doing heinous things. Neither do you suspect it in the case of Titus, who is celebrated like a hero at the beginning. When Titus arrives in Rome, with the bodies of his sons slain on the battlefield, the horrors of war are brought into the theatrical present, at once bloody and glorified.

2 Justifying the Culprits of the Play

Titus Andronicus is the tragic hero of the play, as the most suffering is inflicted on him of all the characters. Against the background that so much has been done to him, it is perhaps easier to sympathize with his thoughts of revenge. However, the fact that he is a tragic hero does not mean that he is an innocent victim, for it could be argued that he is getting the punishment for the murder of Tamora's son. Tamora begged and pleaded with him, but this was a Roman custom that he had to follow. An act prescribed by Roman military custom, and thus nothing personal to the Gothic queen. The acts of vengeance he received in return, however, had nothing to do with tradition. If Titus had a fatal flaw, he would also kill his own son out of a sense of duty and honor, because that is above everything, including family. This is also evident in the scene where he kills his daughter Lavinia so that she does not have to live in shame after her rape. He is not always the most sympathetic character, but he is not a villain either. There is probably a point in this story when Titus realizes that his determination to stick to tradition has gotten him nowhere. Although he lived his life according to the traditions and rules of Rome and service to the state was his top priority, in the end he had to endure unimaginable suffering. The moment he sees his daughter completely destroyed by his enemies, he embarks on a vendetta that leads him away from quiet traditionalism.

If we try to find something good in the bad characters, we should also try to find a bad side in the good characters. So we should ask ourselves if Lavinia has an ugly side that is not being talked about. When Lavinia and Bassianus stumble upon the secret lovers Tamora and Aaron in the middle of the forest, Lavinia makes some snide remarks about Tamora's relationship with her dark-skinned lover and the fact that Tamora has cheated on Saturninus. She also helps her father torture her rapists. I would take this as proof that she is not as perfect as everyone thinks.

2. 1 The Animalization of Man - Speciesism as a Reason for Violence

Since early modern times, humans have tried to distinguish themselves from the animal world and to exist as an independent group. While being human is in itself dependent on animals and one only becomes human through the existence of animals, the human turns out to be the actual animal. Biologically, the human being belongs to the animals. Culturally, the understanding of a special position of humans in the animal kingdom is gaining ground, justified by the human-specific expression of certain abilities. In order to demonstrate his superiority, man exercises power and violence over animals, presents them as objects and takes possession of them. However, this only achieves the opposite, namely that humans become worse animals than those whom they oppress and over whom they want to exercise power.[5] Animals are seen merely as objects of research, food, clothing or toys. They are seen as objects that exist to fulfill people's desires. In the same way, some people are favored over others because of certain prejudices. There is a mistaken assumption that a certain kind or type of person is more important than another. People are excluded and disadvantaged because they are supposedly *different*. One can directly compare the massacres of animals with the extermination of people in war or with the rape of women.

The hunt in which Lavinia is raped is an example of barbarism being at the centre of civilization, as it is portrayed both as a civilized ritual of pleasure for the wealthy upper classes and as the hunting of wild animals. One symbolic image used is that of Lavinia as a woman with a doe's head. The doe is usually associated with innocence and weakness. The tigers, on the other hand - as the two sons of Tamora and the rapists of Lavinia are depicted - are associated with strength and power. The symbolism shows that Lavinia had no chance to protect herself from the two brothers. She is never really seen as a woman but as something that serves men, she is always portrayed as an animal, a tree or a sex symbol. The way her father breaks her neck is more reminiscent of a wounded sparrow than a woman. Even in the scene where Aaron persuades Chiron and Demetrius to rape Lavinia, she is often referred to as a deer. Tamora herself, Lucius concludes, deserves a purely inhuman fate: "her life was beastly and devoid of pity and being dead, let birds on her take pity"[67] But earlier in the play, when the outrages against his family were just beginning, Titus himself declares, "Rome is but a wilderness of tigers"[8]. The atrocity

---

[5] Eric S. Mallin, *Reading Shakespeare in the Movies. Non-Adaptations and Their Meaning.* Texas: Palgrave MacMillan, 2019, 197.
[6] William Shakespeare, *Titus Andronicus.* Hamburg: Dt. Schauspielhaus, 1982, 198-99.
[7] Mallin, *Reading Shakespeare in the Movies*, 199-200.
[8] Shakespeare, *Titus Andronicus*, 3.1.55.

against Lavinia happened outside society, in the wilderness; but the more we think about it, the more the difference between Rome and the wilderness dissolves.

Even the meal at the end of the play - when Titus prepares a pie of Tamora's two sons to serve to their mother - can be assigned a meaning. Throughout the play, body parts are repeatedly dismembered, be it Lavinia's hands and her tongue or Titus' hand. The dismembered body parts are eventually made into a pie or other forms for digestion. Thus the cannibal meal provides the most appropriate conclusion. Cannibalism is

> a device of satire, a trope by which we parody more idealized myths about ourselves, and the banquet in Titus unites in a mocking message the play's collection of physical horrors and functions as a genre indicator, a sign of its serious satire. Only the banquet can offer closure to all the bodies that have been - and still are - opened and openly violated.[9]

Although we are not carnivores by nature, but are supposed to feed on fruits, vegetables, nuts and herbs like common herbivores, it has become a cultural obligation to consume meat. Those who swim against the tide are condemned as always. The slaughter of animals is a huge industry that influences and even determines our choices about what we eat. An industry that makes its money from cruel torture and causes horrors worse than war. Of course, we are guilty as a society if we continue to try to ignore this.[10] We see that education to speciesism and the distinction between humans and animals, is a big factor that leads to all kinds of violence.

2. 2 The Vicious Circle and the Honor of Revenge

Revenge is, of course, the main theme of Titus Andronicus. The play fits perfectly into the category of Elizabethan revenge tragedy and deals with the nature of revenge. Revenge is the solution to the problem of an attack. Someone is wronged and the victim takes revenge, which brings justice and closes the cycle. The problem, however, is that the victim of revenge perceives the revenge as a new and separate wrong and takes revenge himself, which in turn triggers another revenge. This is vividly shown in the final scene when Titus, within a minute, takes revenge on Tamora by killing her, Saturninus kills Titus for killing his wife and Lucius kills Saturninus for killing his father. Lucius is not killed because he is quickly made emperor and everyone who cared about Saturninus is already dead. This sequence of events speeds up the cycle of revenge and makes it ridiculous. The rest of the play consists of Titus taking revenge on Tamora, Chiron and

---

[9] Mallin, *Reading Shakespeare in the Movies*, 201.
[10] Mallin, *Reading Shakespeare in the Movies*, 205.

Demetrius for the revenge they in turn have taken on him for the murder of Alarbus at the beginning of the play. Shakespeare's tragedy ends with the restoration of civil order, for the cycle of revenge is so destructive that it must be interrupted if any form of civilized life is to continue.

Vengeance satisfies man in the sense that it is demanded by his honor. However, the concept of honor has moved away from the republican ideal of integrity and public service and is now much more equated with prestige. This is precisely what Titus means when he speaks of his sons dishonoring him when they oppose him. This identification of male honor with individual prestige means that it has become more subjective. Aaron the Moor considers it a matter of honor to be as bad as possible and is very concerned to avoid virtue and repent. If male honor has changed with the fall of Rome, female honor has not. Lavinia's impeccable chastity is the standard of a woman's virtue, and as Titus and Saturninus confirm in the final scene, she has no life after losing it. In the world of the play, male honor can be satisfied by revenge, but the dishonored woman can only die.

There exists a desire to always do to the other what has been done to oneself and this is the reason why Tamora ignored Lavinia's pleas and entreaties the moment she sent her sons to do an atrocity to her. For just as Lavinia begged in vain, she had once done so herself before Titus. Titus had ignored her while she begged him for her son's life. Tamora already knew at that moment that she must avenge her child, while Titus did not yet know that he would have to avenge his child. It is as if not meeting an evil deed with an evil deed in return is not even a choice, whereas one could also simply try to show understanding for the suffering of others, and recognize common ground among them. In the scene where Tamora appears before Titus as Revenge, Titus embraces not only Revenge's disguise, but also Tamora herself, which is an allusion to how blinded with desire for revenge the two characters are to realize that they have some things in common.

3 The Meaning of the Violence done to Lavinia

Titus' daughter Lavinia does not have it easy in Titus Andronicus. After her marriage, she is brutally raped by Demetrius and Chiron, who also cut out her tongue and chop off her hands so that she cannot tell anyone what happened to her. Marcus does not want old Titus to see his beloved daughter in such a terrible state, but under the circumstances he has no choice. But before he shows Titus what has happened to Lavinia, he warns him that the sight will break his heart. Marcus leads Lavinia to Titus and warns him that this was once his daughter. The fact that he uses the past tense here is very telling. It strongly suggests that Lavinia was once Titus' daughter, but since she was so horribly raped and mutilated, that is no longer the case. The prevailing morality at the time was that a woman who had been raped was dishonored by her injury and was therefore less of a woman. Physical integrity was considered an important part of a person's character, and Lavinia's mutilation undoubtedly called her own integrity into question. Markus' use of the past tense is not an oversight, but an expression of values that were widespread among the Roman population.

Let us try to understand the violence done to Lavinia in Shakespeare's cruelest play. Karen Cunningham argues in her essay *Scars can Witness* that Lavinia rises in her role in the play after her rape and the cutting out of her tongue. She goes from being a minor character to a major character. One could say that the suffering gives her a higher value. The importance of her body serves both to highlight her powerlessness and to show her intertwining of sexuality and criminality. She becomes a victim, which also changes the focus of the play from a more politically oriented work to a crime thriller. The political discussion moves into the background and the search for a solution to the mystery of who caused Lavinia her suffering comes to the fore. The Andronici try to interpret Lavinia's body and make sense of her mutilation. Lavinia's mutilated body can be interpreted in multiple and complex ways, and it becomes clear that Shakespeare is pointing here to the problematic nature of court cases.

3. 1. The symbolism behind the Mutilation

In court, finding out the truth is a sure way to establish justice through the jury. This variation is in direct contrast to the time when the corpse alone served as evidence. To find a deeper meaning behind Lavinia's existence, it is helpful to look at how people were violently abused to find out the truth and how the body itself had a greater meaning. *Trial by Ordeal* is a decision supposedly brought about by a supernatural sign, which was also used in the Middle Ages to find the truth in a legal dispute. Behind this is the idea that only a god or a power of fate as the highest authority in an existential decision-making process could deliver an infallible verdict. It was the most important means to determine whether a crime had been committed and to convict the criminal. The guilt or innocence of the accused was determined by dangerous or painful trials that were believed to be under divine control. Shakespeare uses the theme of torture to give meaning to physical trials. When Titus Andronicus first saw his mutilated daughter, he wondered what it meant. Whatever it may stand for - whether as a symbol of patience or as a sign of sorrow and grief - it definitely shows the higher significance of the body over all other existing forms of expression.[11] Lavinia's tongue has been cut off so that she cannot speak of her grief, and her hands have been cut off so that she cannot write down the names of the perpetrators, but despite her silence she is meaningful, and even through this she acquires her true great significance. In her we recognize a time when silence was more meaningful than speech.[12] After Lavinia loses her hands and her tongue and becomes traumatized, she transforms into the ideal woman, as Rome of the time would have wanted. She is mute, obedient and chaste, for chaste means that she retains her purity even though she loses her virginity.

Apart from the meaning as sexual assault, the term rape is given another meaning, namely at the moment when Saturninus says that Bassianus should repent of this rape, whereas Bassianus replies, "'Rape' call you it, my lord, to seize my own, / My true betrothed love and now my wife?"[13]. At this moment we realize that Lavinia has not only been raped in the forest by Chiron and Demetrius, but already in Rome. Even here, Lavinia is already silencing herself and only quietly listening to Bassianus, although in this case no one is forcing her to be silent. The comparison to the rape in the forest cannot be ignored in this respect. Lavinia's silence and her dismembered body show how people abdicate their right to speak in order to give power to men and monarchs.

At the beginning of the play, Lavinia defies her father's authority to marry her to Saturninus and instead gives her hand to Bassianus, a man she had previously agreed to marry her. A little while after, the Goths bring her back to the stage after amputating her hands, cutting out her tongue and raping her. Such a violent fate visually reinforces the sense that the underlying struggle for supremacy in Titus, whether the struggle for Rome or the struggle for Lavinia, is being played out through mutilated rituals of consent. Lavinia's severed hands and tongue further dramatize the loss of consent by relocating internal and psychological injuries to conspicuous limbs.

The succession of gruesome acts of violence that took place in the forest contain a common and repetitive symbolism: Tamora's sons throw the body of Lavinia's fiancé into a hole in the ground; Aaron, Tamora's lover ensures that Lavinia's brothers fall into a hole; meanwhile, Chiron and Demetrius penetrate Lavinia; Titus ensures that Chiron and Demetrius enter their mother's body through the meal. This repetitive image is a direct comparison to a dark hole in which the downfall of the Andronici awaits, devouring the

---

[11] Karen Cunningham, *Scars Can Witness*, in: Katherine Anne Ackley, *Women and Violence in Literature - An Essay Collection.* New York u.a.: Garland, 1990, 145.
[12] Cunningham, *Scars Can Witness*, 155.
[13] Shakespeare, *Titus Andronicus*, 12.

people within. Quintus also describes the mouth of the pit as stained with blood, making it an image of the assault on Lavinia that is taking place as he speaks.

3. 2 The Symbolism behind the Rape

When a woman has lost her chastity, whether by her own choice or by violent rape, the result is the same: by losing her chastity, she becomes a common horror, and because she is defined by her relationship with men, she reflects badly on her family, especially her husband or father. The moment Lavinia begs Tamora to kill her, there is a widely held view that rape is a fate worse than death for a chaste woman. Lavinia is well aware that in losing her virginity she also loses her honor, and that this is precisely the intention of Tamora, Chiron and Demetrius.[14]

Although we have all seen horror films before, and films in which blood flows, the specificity of the horror of Lavinia's rape does not escape any reader - then or now.

Apart from her dishonor, the rape had another purpose, namely that it thus also *castrated* the male members of her family. The reason for this is that the men, who were supposed to be the protectors of the family, failed in their task and could not protect the purity of their wives, sisters or children. In this way it could even be seen as a greater dishonor to Titus than it was to Lavinia. Here, the father loses his power just as he did at the moment when Aaron chopped off his hand. The symbol of dishonor and loss of power that is the raped and mutilated Lavinia must be removed from the Andronici family before healing can occur.[15]

Tamora, as a former queen of the Goths, reclaims her own power and shows Titus to be an impotent, castrated and dishonored man. Her evil deed turns the order of men raping women and power holders taking over the wives of their victims upside down. Here it is she who orders the child of her victim Titus to be raped.

At the end of Act Five, when Lucius orders Tamora's corpse to be left to the predators, he reflects the long-held belief that the unchaste woman is being transformed from a creature inferior to man, but human, into a creature worse than the beasts. Tamora's decision to follow her lusts and desire for revenge led to her death, the death of all but one of her children, and ultimately the fall of the Roman Empire.[16] Titus murders Lavinia with the words, "die die Lavinia and thy shame with thee, And with thy shame thy Father

---

[14] Lee A. Ritscher, *The Semiotics or Rape in Renaissance English Literature*. NewYork: Peter Lang Publishing, 2009, 86.
[15] Ritscher, *The Semiotics or Rape in Renaissance English Literature,* 91.
[16] Ritscher, *The Semiotics or Rape in Renaissance English Literature,* 92.

sorrow die."[17] Titus proves with his words that his daughter has brought shame on her family, and that this shame can only be removed by her death.[18]

4 Understanding for Titus the Cruel Murderer

The spectacle is unforgettable: Titus and Lavinia leave the stage in Act Four, Titus carrying the severed head of a son and Lavinia taking her father's severed hand in her mouth. Even when they have left the stage, other characters cruelly take their tragedy in their stride. Aaron Lucius, for example, confesses his evil deeds and cannot resist recounting the details.

Amidst the ruins, Titus, the former honorable warrior, can no longer endure all that has been done to him, all the shame, the sorrow, the loss of his honor, and thus he goes mad.[19] It is clear that he has gone mad in the face of the bloodshed, and at the same time he does what he can to save what is left of his family. When he asks Aaron to cut off his hand, he does so in the hope of saving the lives of his two sons. When he realizes that his sons have been executed anyway, he reacts by laughing - a sign of his madness, while Aaron probably thinks Titus has lost his mind. His relatives also think he is mad when he asks them to shoot arrows into the sky to ask the gods for revenge. When Tamora disguises herself as Revenge, she may think Titus is crazy, but he reveals to the audience that he knows exactly who she and her sons are, disguised as Rape and Murder. So we see that even when he goes mad, he still knows everything, just as he did when he murdered his daughter Lavinia, appearing cold-blooded and insane. Maybe Lavinia wants to be dead after what happened to her, or Titus wants to erase her shame, but first of all he kills her on purpose to let the others know that he knows she was raped. The scene where Titus reveals to Tamora that she is eating her sons' remains also shows Titus' madness and calculation.

The violent outbursts in Titus Andronicus seem completely gratuitous and only serve to shock the audience or the reader. Titus kills his own children for reasons that seem completely senseless to us. He stabs his own son Mutius to death just because he stands in his way, and kills his daughter to free her from her shame. In the face of these acts, Aaron shocks us by caring for and trying to protect his newborn child. Aaron, in his last breath, repents of every good deed he has done and does not commit another murder.[20]

---

[17] Shakespeare, *Titus Andronicus*, 45-46.
[18] Ritscher, *The Semiotics or Rape in Renaissance English Literature,* 93.
[19] Foakes, *Shakespeare and Violence*, 56.
[20] Foakes, *Shakespeare and Violence*, 57.

I would still answer the question of whether Titus is a hero or a villain with hero. Titus gave his life and that of his sons to serve Rome and was rewarded with betrayal. Lavinia did not deserve what was done to her under any circumstances. Alarbus' sacrifice was not personal, but part of the war. Had the roles been reversed, it would have been the same. Titus or a son of Titus would have been sacrificed to the one the Goths worshipped. The rape and mutilation of Lavinia was personal. As a father, Titus had to take revenge. The plot is set in ancient Rome, but selfishness and competition, violence and revenge define life across the centuries.

5 The Normality of Violence across the Centuries

The failed civilization in Rome is not contrasted with the animalistic, but presented as if it were just another version of the animalistic.[21] Overall, the work does not allow us to find a direct answer to the question of what all the violence is about. We know that everything has a deeper meaning behind it, but have to be content with not understanding it all.[22] Perhaps some of the violence perpetrated has to do with insufficient care, as mothers are very conspicuously absent from the text. The lack of mothers, could have created a contempt, disrespect and also misogyny shown towards women. Both women in the text, Lavinia and Tamora, are horribly abused. What happens to Titus is horrific, but what is done to women are things that would not even occur to you.[23]

The British living in the Elizabethan age at the time of Shakespeare were used to the sight of blood. To see people being publicly executed and the like. Just as we watch horror films for fun today, they went to public executions of people for fun.[24] The horrors depicted in the play, shocking as they may be to the kind, gentle culture we think we are, would probably not have shocked an audience that was regularly entertained by violence. William Shakespeare's Titus Andronicus criticizes paternalism and highlights its dangers. Paternalism means the power of men to oppress women and secure male domination. Women who interrupt this male fantasy of complete docility and obedience are severely punished. In the specific case of Titus Andronicus, the tradition of paternalism manifests itself in Titus giving Lavinia to Saturninus as his bride, unaware that Lavinia and Bassianus are betrothed to each other.[25] The violence against women in the play only

---

[21] Mallin, *Reading Shakespeare in the Movies*, 214.
[22] Mallin, *Reading Shakespeare in the Movies*, 218.
[23] Mallin, *Reading Shakespeare in the Movies*, 224.
[24] Ritscher, *The Semiotics or Rape in Renaissance English Literature*, 69.
[25] Ritscher, *The Semiotics or Rape in Renaissance English Literature*, 70.

serves to underscore the ultimate fate that awaits women who speak in early modern English revenge tragedy, which is death.[26]

As a woman who has lost her exchange value, both through her imperfect marriage to Bassianus and her rape, Lavinia's enforced silence only reinforces the sense that she should be seen as a sexual object, even though she arouses the pity of her male family members.[27] In Titus Andronicus, restoring order to the households of the Roman emperor and the Andronici family requires the death of all who participate in the female desire for revenge. Civilisation and barbarism are not separate but intertwined.

---

[26] Ritscher, *The Semiotics or Rape in Renaissance English Literature*, 72.
[27] Ritscher, *The Semiotics or Rape in Renaissance English Literature*, 73.

Bibliography

Primary Source

Shakespeare, William, *Titus Andronicus*. Hamburg: Dt. Schauspielhaus, 1982.

Secondary Sources

Foakes, R. A., *Shakespeare and Violence*. Cambridge: Cambridge UP, 2003.

Ritscher, Lee A., *The Semiotics or Rape in Renaissance English Literature*. NewYork: Peter Lang Publishing, 2009.

Mallin, Eric S., *Reading Shakespeare in the Movies. Non-Adaptations and Their Meaning*. Texas: Palgrave MacMillan, 2019.

Cunningham, Karen, *Scars Can Witness*, in: Anne Ackley, Katherine, *Women and Violence in Literature - An Essay Collection*. New York u.a.: Garland, 1990.

YOUR KNOWLEDGE HAS VALUE

- We will publish your bachelor's and
  master's thesis, essays and papers

- Your own eBook and book -
  sold worldwide in all relevant shops

- Earn money with each sale

Upload your text at www.GRIN.com
and publish for free